This book was purchased with
funds generously donated by

Ms. Joyce Marlin

In addition to being a sponsor to our 2nd Annual
Fun Run/Walk, Joyce was Senior Branch
Librarian at the Concord Library
from 1979—1993

BEETLES

BY KATHLEEN DERZIPILSKI

BENCHMARK BOOKS

MARSHALL CAVENDISH
NEW YORK

Series Consultant
James Doherty
General Curator
Bronx Zoo, New York

Thanks to Paul Zabarouskas of the Bronx Zoo for his expert reading of this manuscript.

Benchmark Books
Marshall Cavendish
99 White Plains Road
Tarrytown, NY 10591–9001
www.marshallcavendish.com

Library of Congress Cataloging-in-Publication Data

Derzipilski, Kathleen.
Beetles / by Kathleen Derzipilski.
v. cm. – (Animals, animals)
Includes bibliographical references (p. 44) and index.
Contents: What is a beetle – The beetle's body – How beetles grow – How beetles live – Beetles and people.
ISBN 0–7614–1751–6
1. Beetles–Juvenile literature. [1. Beetles.] I. Title. II. Series.
QL576.2.D47 2004
595.76–dc22
2003024841

Photo Research by Joan Meisel
Cover Photo: Paul A. Zahl/Getty Images

Photographs in this book are used by permission and through the courtesy of: *Corbis:* Michael & Patricia Fogden, 14, 16, 26, 30; Gallo Images,
28; Anthony Bannister/Gallo Images, 31; Corbis Royalty Free, 34; George D. Lepp, 35. *Getty:* GeoStock, 4; Daniel Bosler, 32. *Peter Arnold, Inc.:* Hans
Pfletschinger: 6 (center), 7 (bottom), 12, 15, 18, 20, 21, 24, 39, 40; Martin Harvey, 8, 22–23; John R. Macgregor, 7 (top); Michael J. Doolittle, 10;
James Gerholdt, 37. *Photo Researchers, Inc.:* Nigel Cattlin, 6 (top); Kent Wood, 6 (bottom); E.R. Degginger, 7 (bottom).

Printed in China
1 3 5 6 4 2

CONTENTS

1
WHAT IS A BEETLE?

A ladybug lands on your arm. Just as you start to look closely, it lifts its hard red wings, stretches the pair of thin wings underneath, and takes off. Those hard upper wings tell you that the ladybug is a beetle.

Beetles are a type of insect. Like all insects, the beetle's body is in three separate parts. It has a head, a thorax, and an abdomen. The body is covered and protected by a tough *exoskeleton*, its outer skeleton. The beetle's colors may be brown, black, red, orange, yellow, blue, or green. These colors may be dull or bright, plain, or arranged in striking patterns. Beetles range in size from being as tiny as a pen point to being large enough to fill your hand.

Of all the animals on Earth, insects are the most numerous and have the most *species*, or kinds. There are about a million species of insects, and about 350,000 of these are beetles. Each year, scientists find and describe several more species of beetles.

THE LADYBUG IS ONE OF THE MANY SPECIES OF BEETLES.

BEETLE SPECIES

SHOWN HERE ARE SIX SPECIES OF BEETLE.
LENGTH IS FOR AN ADULT BEETLE FROM HEAD TO TAIL.

**Giant stag beetle
1 to 1 1/2 inches (30 to 40 mm)**

**Tiger beetle
1/2 inch (13 mm)**

**Spotted cucumber beetle
1/4 inch (7 mm)**

Firefly
1/2 inch (13 mm)

Rose chafer beetle
1/3 to 2/5 inches (8 to 10 mm)

Giant water scavenger beetle
1 inch (25 mm)

THE RHINOCEROS BEETLE LIVES IN THE DAMP FOREST.

Beetles live nearly everywhere on Earth, from the equator to the polar regions, and in a variety of *habitats*. They can survive in the driest deserts or on snowy mountains. Beetles may live in the warm, moist litter of forests and meadows. Some beetles live on the surface of quiet ponds, while others need the bubbly waters of a swiftly running stream. They live in the fur and feathers of other animals and in their nests. A few live on sandy beaches and cliffs, and in the darkness of caves.

Beetles are everywhere and yet they often go unnoticed. For much of their lives, many species stay hidden from view underground or inside plants and trees. They live unseen under rocks or among dead leaves. Adult beetles may be active only during the warm summer months and then only at night. Many beetles are so tiny they are easily overlooked.

2
THE BEETLE'S BODY

The beetle's exoskeleton is both flexible and hard. These qualities let a beetle slip through tight or rough places without getting hurt. Even when it flies into things or drops to the ground, the beetle escapes injury. Inside, the soft organs stay protected.

The exoskeleton is divided into plates connected by flexible tissues. Muscles attach to small folds and ridges inside the exoskeleton. The muscles control all of the beetle's movements.

Sense organs in the exoskeleton detect smells, touch and vibrations, light, temperature, and dampness. Beetles use this information to find food and mates, and to stay safe.

Most beetles have two *compound eyes* bulging on either side of the head. Compound eyes have many lenses and are good at seeing movement. Such sharp vision is important to beetles that fly and hunt. Beetles that do not fly or that live in the dark have small compound eyes, or they have *simple eyes* with one lens only, or no eyes at all.

THE UNUSUAL SHAPE OF THE LEGS GIVES THIS BEETLE THE NAME OF FROG BEETLE.

THE SHARP JAWS OF THE LONG-HORNED BEETLE CAN BITE INTO WOOD AND BARK.

A pair of antennae is also on the head. Antennae are sometimes called feelers. They have organs sensitive to smells and touch and are always moving. The beetle uses them to test the air and the ground for scents and vibrations.

At the front of the head are the mouthparts with curved jaws that close like pincers. Beetles such as lady-bugs, which feed on other insects, pierce their prey with these sharp jaws. Through a small hole at the tip, they inject a liquid to dissolve the victim's insides. Then they suck in the liquid food. Beetles that eat algae have bristles on their jaws. The bristles help beetles collect food by scraping it off of plants.

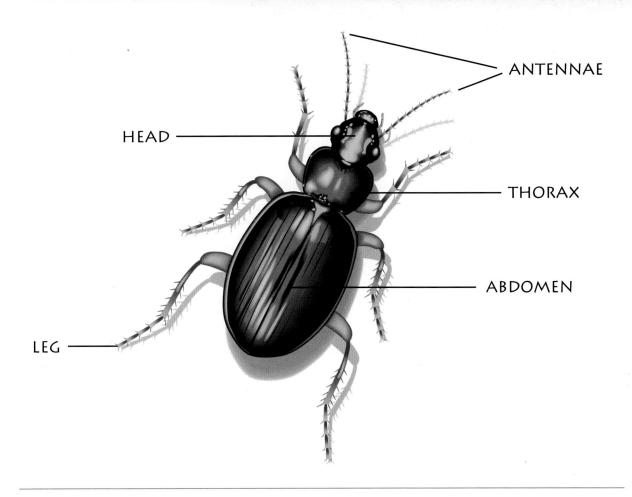

ANTENNAE

HEAD

THORAX

ABDOMEN

LEG

LIKE ALL INSECTS, BEETLES HAVE A HARD EXOSKELETON, A THREE-PART BODY, THREE PAIRS OF LEGS, AND TWO ANTENNAE.

SCULPTURE ON THE BODY

THE SURFACE OF A BEETLE MAY BE DECORATED WITH BUMPS AND DENTS. A PATTERN OF WRINKLES, RIDGES, GROOVES, OR PITS MAY RUN OVER THE WINGS AND LEGS. SPINES AND HORNS JUT FROM THE HEAD. ON A BEETLE, ALL THESE FORMS ARE KNOWN AS ITS SCULPTURE.

The thorax is behind the head. It has three segments, and each segment has a pair of legs. Each of the second and third segments has a pair of wings. The hard forewings protect the thin hind wings folded under–neath them. To prepare for flight, the beetle warms up its wing muscles. Then, it raises the forewings out of the way. The hind wings unfold and beat rapidly. Some species of beetles, though, cannot fly.

The shape of the legs and the feet tell how the beetle uses them. Beetles that run over the open ground have long, thin legs. Scarab beetles dig in the dirt and have short, broad legs thick with spurs and hairs. The hairy legs of diving beetles help them to paddle through water. The beetle's legs and the feet also detect vibrations and touch. The feet pick up smells, too.

IN FLIGHT, THE FOREWINGS ARE LIFTED SO THE HIND WINGS ARE FREE TO
OPEN AND MOVE.

COLORFUL FOREWINGS COVER THE ABDOMEN OF THIS FUNGUS BEETLE.

Insects have their own way of bringing oxygen to their cells. Instead of passing through lungs or gills, air enters their body through tiny tubes. The openings to the tubes are on the abdomen and the thorax. Inside, the tubes branch out to bring oxygen to every cell.

3
HOW BEETLES GROW

Insects grow in stages in a process called *metamorphosis*. The life cycle of beetles has four stages and is called complete metamorphosis. The beetle changes from an egg to a *larva* to a *pupa*, and then to an adult.

Beetles begin life as eggs. The eggs may hatch in a few days. If they are laid in late summer or in the fall, the eggs wait until winter has passed to hatch. The eggs hatch into larva, sometimes called grubs. In appearance, beetle larvae resemble caterpillars. They have a head with strong jaws and a long body. Six short legs usually grow from the thorax. Larvae have big appetites. As they eat and grow, they become too big for their exoskeletons and must *molt*. The outgrown covering is shed and replaced with a new, larger one.

IF THE WEATHER IS HOT, THESE BEETLE EGGS WILL HATCH INTO LARVA IN FOUR DAYS.

A BEETLE LARVA EATS AS MUCH AS IT CAN BEFORE IT BECOMES A PUPA.

When the larva is fully grown, it finds a place where it can rest. It molts one last time and the new covering hardens into the case of a pupa. During this stage, the beetle changes into its adult form. The beetle may stay as a pupa through the winter. When it is ready, the adult beetle breaks out of the dry case.

THE OLD CASE OF THE LADYBUG'S PUPA LIES BESIDE THE NEW ADULT.

Many adult beetles eat, but unlike the larvae they do not grow. They need energy to find mates and to produce eggs and sperm. Beetles that live to the next year need to build stores of fat for the winter.

A PAIR OF DUNG BEETLES ON A BROOD BALL. THE MALE MAKES A BALL OF DUNG, WHICH IS OFFERED TO THE FEMALE. IF SHE ACCEPTS, THEY ROLL THE BALL AWAY TOGETHER AND MATE.

SOLDIER BEETLES EAT OTHER INSECTS. WHILE THEY WAIT FOR PREY, THEY MAY FEED ON FLOWERS BUT THEY DO NOT DAMAGE THE PLANTS.

Male and female beetles find each other in various ways. They may meet when they are both eating the same food. Male fireflies signal to the females with a pattern of flashing light. Other beetles use *pheromones* to announce their presence. Pheromones are chemicals with distinct odors that insects use to communicate.

24

A beetle that is ready to mate produces a cloud of pheromones. Beetles are very sensitive to these scents and will follow them a great distance to find a mate.

The male and the female form a pair and the male passes his sperm to the female. The female carries the sperm until she is ready to lay the eggs. She lays the eggs in a protected area and near where the larvae will have food.

After laying the eggs, most females leave. Some beetles protect their eggs from being eaten by smearing them with an unpleasant tasting liquid. Water beetles make a cocoon to protect the eggs and to keep them afloat. In only a few species do the females keep watch over the eggs or feed the larvae once the eggs hatch.

The entire life cycle can take three weeks or some-times two or three years to complete, depending on the species and the weather. In many species, the beetle spends most of its life as a larva. This is when it eats the most and grows.

4
HOW BEETLES LIVE

What a beetle eats and how it goes through its life cycle depend on its *habitat*, the place where it lives. A habitat includes all the animals and plants living in an area, as well as the soil, water, and weather.

Mold beetles live in warm, moist places such as rotting logs, leaf mold, and animal nests. They feed on the molds that grow there. The female bark beetle knows by smell which trees in a forest are old, weakened by drought, or dying and seeks this type of tree in which to lay its eggs.

In the summer, June bugs feed at night on leaves, fruit, and flowers. In the day they burrow in the ground. They also lay their eggs in the ground. When June bugs hatch, the larvae will be close to their own food, the roots. Adult blister beetles and their larvae also eat different foods.

THIS SCARAB BEETLE POLLINATES FLOWERS WHEN IT WALKS OVER THEM.

A LADYBUG SUCKS THE JUICES FROM AN APHID.

The adults eat leaves, stems, and flowers. They lay their eggs in the ground near the underground nests of bees. The young larvae find their way into the bee nest. In the nest, the beetle larvae eat the bee eggs and larvae.

The tiger beetle is a hunter. It runs down insects and small animals and grabs them between large, sharp jaws. The tiger beetle likes to sun itself in an open sandy area. Here, it has a clear view of any prey that walks within its reach. The tiger beetle larva lives in burrows in the sand. It anchors itself to the sides of the burrow and raises its head just above the opening. The tiger beetle larva must wait for prey to walk over it, but it waits ready and with its jaws open.

Beetles themselves are food. They are eaten by birds, frogs, toads, lizards, fish, and other beetles and insects. For defense, some beetles use bad tastes and smells. A frightened darkling beetle points its abdomen in the air and gives off a stinky gas. When a blister beetle is picked

THE ANCESTORS OF TODAY'S BEETLES HAVE BEEN FOUND IN FOSSILS DATING TO THE PERMIAN AGE, ABOUT 280 MILLION YEARS AGO. FISH AND REPTILES WERE ALREADY LIVING ON EARTH, BUT IT WAS LONG BEFORE ANY DINOSAURS, MAMMALS, OR BIRDS WOULD APPEAR.

up it "bleeds" from the joints in its legs. The "blood" stings and can raise blisters. Threatened ladybugs also bleed a dark yellow blood from their leg joints. Colorful beetles often taste bad. Predators soon learn to leave these irritating beetles alone.

THE SPOTTED FOREWINGS HELP THIS BEETLE TO BLEND INTO ITS SURROUNDINGS.

THE BRIGHT COLOR IS A MESSAGE THAT SAYS THIS BEETLE IS POISONOUS.

Most beetles avoid predators by hiding. Some beetles live in out–of–the–way places or are camouflaged by their colors and patterns. Many beetles are active at night when predators cannot see them. Or beetles escape by simply fleeing. They fly or run away, or pull in their legs and drop to the ground.

5
BEETLES AND PEOPLE

People are fascinated by beetles. They marvel at the beauty of their colors and forms. They search for beetles in their gardens and in the wild. They set up lights and a sheet to attract beetles that come out at night. Scientists study beetles to better understand nature and its life forms. By comparing the beetles in museum collections and the beetles found today, they begin to learn how species change.

But to other people, beetles are ugly. The sight of a beetle makes them nervous. They run from beetles or squash them. Beetles that are pests are especially hated. They get into homes and warehouses and eat flour, grain, and wool. In fields and gardens, beetles can weaken plants and ruin a harvest. Cotton growers worry that boll weevils will invade their fields. These destructive beetles

CHILDREN OBSERVE A BEETLE.

COTTONWOOD BORER BEETLES PREFER TO EAT COTTONWOOD TREES BUT WILL ALSO USE WILLOWS AND POPLARS. THESE BEETLES CAN CAUSE SIGNIFICANT DAMAGE TO TREES.

SINCE ARRIVING IN THE U.S. FROM MEXICO IN 1892, THE BOLL WEEVIL HAS COST COTTON GROWERS NEARLY $14 BILLION. AGGRESSIVE PROGRAMS WERE LAUNCHED THAT SUCCESSFULLY ELIMINATED BOLL WEEVILS FROM SEVERAL COTTON-PRODUCING STATES.

lay their eggs in the flower buds of the cotton plant. The larvae eat the flower buds and so prevent the plant from producing cotton fibers. A cotton field destroyed by boll weevils is a costly failure.

Growers and ranchers have used certain beetles to their advantage. In the late 1800s, citrus orchards in California were overrun with scale insects. The growers imported ladybugs from Australia that quickly ate the scale insects.

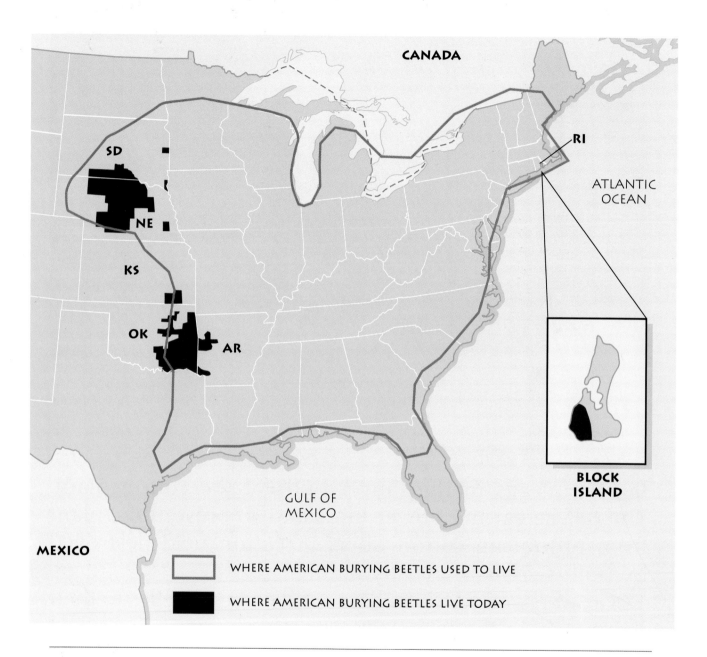

CANADA

RI

ATLANTIC
OCEAN

SD

NE

KS

OK

AR

BLOCK
ISLAND

GULF OF
MEXICO

MEXICO

☐ WHERE AMERICAN BURYING BEETLES USED TO LIVE

■ WHERE AMERICAN BURYING BEETLES LIVE TODAY

THIS MAP SHOWS THE RANGE OF THE AMERICAN BURYING BEETLE IN THE
PAST AND TODAY.

TODAY, IT IS RARE TO FIND AN AMERICAN BURYING BEETLE.

Since then, ladybugs have been used worldwide to control pests such as aphids and scale. Cattle ranchers recognize the good work of scarab beetles. Scarabs bury dung and help keep down the number of flies.

But even with the great number of beetles, some species are endangered. Among the endangered beetles in the United States is the American burying beetle. At one time, this beetle was widespread in the grasslands and woodlands of the eastern half of North America.

Now, a few beetles remain on Block Island, Rhode Island, and in small areas of Oklahoma, Nebraska, Arkansas, Kansas, and South Dakota.

Burying beetles are shiny black with bright orange spots. They eat *carrion*, the decaying body of a dead animal. These interesting beetles also lay their eggs in carrion and feed their larvae from it. To prepare the carrion for the eggs, a female and a male burying beetle bring the *carcass* to a soft burying place. They scoop out the dirt from under it and bury it deep enough so flies cannot lay eggs in it. Then they roll the carcass into a ball. The female lays the eggs near the carcass, and the parents stay with the eggs. When the larvae hatch, the parents feed them until the larvae can begin feeding on the carcass themselves. So much care for the young is rare among beetle parents.

Like all animals, the American burying beetle helps to keep nature in balance. When it buries a decaying animal, the beetle puts nutrients into the soil where plants can use them. The American burying beetle also helps to reduce the number of flies. It eats fly eggs and maggots, and clears the ground of dead animals that flies would use to lay their eggs.

IN ADDITION TO POTATO CROPS, THE POTATO BEETLE CAN SERIOUSLY DAMAGE
TOMATO, EGGPLANT, AND PEPPER PLANTS.

THE DIFFERENT SHAPES AND HABITS OF BEETLES ARE EXAMPLES OF NATURE'S GREAT VARIETY.

Many things have brought about the loss of the American burying beetle, all of which have been caused by humans. The landscape of North America has changed. The mice and birds used by the American burying beetle are not as abundant as they once were. The soft ground needed to bury the carrion is not as easy for them to find.

State and federal laws are in place to protect this rare species. To increase the number of American burying beetles, they are raised in captivity and then released into the wild. People are hopeful that with help this beetle will be able to survive.

Beetles have an important place in a great variety of habitats. They can be found everywhere as eggs, pupae, larvae, or adults. How beetles live affects all the plants and animals living with them.

carcass: The body of a dead animal.

carrion: The decaying body of an animal used for food.

compound eye: A type of insect eye that has many lenses.

exoskeleton: A hard outer structure that provides protection and support; an external skeleton.

habitats: Places where animals live that provide everything they need to survive.

larva (plural larvae): The growing stage of a beetle. Also called grub or worm.

metamorphosis: The series of changes an insect goes through in its growth from egg to adult.

molt: To shed an exoskeleton when it becomes too small.

pheromones: Chemicals made by insects to announce their presence.

pupa (plural pupae): The resting stage during complete metamorphosis, between larva and adult, when a beetle turns into an adult.

simple eyes: Eyes having only one lens.

species: A single type of living thing.

F I N D O U T M O R E

BOOKS

Bernhard, Emery. *Ladybug.* New York: Holiday House, 1992.

Hogner, Dorothy Childs. *Water Beetles.* New York: Thomas Y. Crowell, 1963.

Johnson, Sylvia A. *Beetles.* Minneapolis: Lerner Publications, 1982.

Patent, Dorothy Hinshaw, and Paul C. Schroeder. *Beetles and How They Live.* New York: Holiday House, 1978.

Walker, Sally M. *Fireflies.* Minneapolis, MN: Lerner Publications, 2001.

WEB SITES

The Tree of Life

tolweb.org/tree?group=Coleoptera&contgroup=Endopterygota

Iowa State University Image Gallery

www.ent.iastate.edu/imagegal/coleoptera/

Exploring California's Insects

www.bugpeople.org/taxa/Coleoptera/OrderColeopteraPage.htm

University of California, Berkeley
Museum of Paleontology

www.ucmp.berkeley.edu/arthropoda/uniramia/coleoptera.html

The Tiger Beetles of Nebraska

entomology.unl.edu/nebraska_tigers/tigers_home.htm

ABOUT THE AUTHOR

Kathleen Derzipilski first saw beetles in the flower garden at her childhood home in California. She has also observed beetles walking on canyon paths and at night while sitting on the porch. She shares her discoveries with her neighbors and friends.

INDEX

Page numbers for illustrations are in **boldface.**